W9-ARG-907

PERSONAL BEST

BASKETBALL

CLIVE GIFFORD

PowerKiDS press™

New York

Published in 2009 by The Rosen Publishing Group Inc.
29 East 21st Street, New York, NY 10010

Copyright © 2009 Wayland/The Rosen Publishing Group, Inc.

All rights reserved. No part of this book may be reproduced in any form without permission from the publisher, except by a reviewer.

First Edition

Managing Editor: Rasha Elsaeed
Produced by Tall Tree Ltd
Editor: Jon Richards
Designer: Ben Ruocco
Photographer: Michael Wicks
Consultant: Steve Darlow

Library of Congress Cataloging-in-Publication Data

Gifford, Clive.
  Basketball / Clive Gifford. — 1st ed.
      p. cm. — (Personal best)
  Includes index.
  ISBN 978-1-4042-4444-3 (library binding)
  1. Basketball—Juvenile literature. I. Title.
  GV885.G48 2008
  796.323—dc22

                              2007042989

Picture credits
All photographs taken by Michael Wicks, except;
Cover Dreamstime.com/Chris Ryan, 5 Larry W. Smith/epa/Corbis

Disclaimer
In the preparation of this book, care has been exercised with regard to advice, activities and techniques. However, when the reader is learning or engaged in a sport or utilizing a piece of equipment, the reader should get advice from an expert and follow the manufacturer's instructions. The publisher cannot be, and is not liable for, any loss or injury the reader may sustain.

Manufactured in China

CONTENTS

WHAT IS BASKETBALL?

Basketball is an all-action team sport. Five players on each team dribble and pass a basketball around a court, trying to get into a position to shoot at the basket and score points. The team with the most points at the end of the game wins. If the scores are level at the end, one or more periods of overtime are played until one team wins.

A coach gathers his players together during a time out. Each team in a basketball game has a set number of time outs, each lasting up to a minute. Apart from providing rest and a short break in play, a time out lets a coach and his players discuss team tactics.

DIFFERENT RULES

Elite basketball players are professionals and massive stars with competitions held at the Olympic games for both men and women. Olympic basketball, the World Championships, and many other national and regional competitions are played to rules set by the International Basketball Federation (FIBA). In North America, elite college basketball and the National Basketball Association (NBA) play to slightly different rules—some of these differences are listed on page 5.

FAST AND FURIOUS

Run by a pair of referees and other officials including scorers and timekeepers, basketball is played at a quick pace with the emphasis on incredible athleticism and reactions, fast moves, and equally fast scoring. When a team gains possession of the ball, they have just 24 seconds in which to take a shot, otherwise possession of the ball passes to the other team. The time a team has left is usually displayed on a large shot clock by the court. Players on the court can be swapped around at any time with any of the substitutes on the teams' benches. This means that a player can be substituted and brought back on as often as a coach likes.

This player makes a shot standing outside of the three-point line (see page 7). If the shot is successful, he will score three points. Regular shots from inside the three-point line are worth two points, and free throws (see page 21) are worth one point each.

Team play is a vital part of basketball. In the sequence on the left, an attacking player in black has run past the defenderr marking him. He is now clear to receive a pass from a teammate and score.

Key differences between NBA and FIBA rules of basketball

	NBA	FIBA
Game duration:	4 x 12 minute quarters	4 x 10 minute quarters
Time outs allowed:	7 per game	2 in first two quarters, 3 in second two
Player foul limit:	6	5
Who calls time out:	Coach or player	Coach only
Time allowed for a free throw:	10 seconds	5 seconds
Number of officials on the court:	3	2

Players from the Cleveland Cavaliers and the San Antonio Spurs compete under the basket during the NBA playoffs.

PLAYING THE GAME

A basketball court has a series of markings. The court is divided into two halves, and the end your team is defending is known as the back court. Play continues inside the court boundaries until there is a violation, a foul (see page 20), a time out, the ball leaves the court, or the playing period ends.

COURT RULES

The sidelines and backlines of the court are considered out of play. If the ball or a player holding the ball touches one of these lines, then he or she is out of play. However, if the ball is in midair and over the sideline or backline, then it is not out of play until it has hit the ground.

When a team gets the ball in the back court, they have just eight seconds to get the ball across the halfway line. When it is over the halfway line and in the front court, the team cannot take the ball back into the back court. If either of the above offenses occurs, one of the referees will signal a violation and possession of the ball will pass to the opposition. There are a number of other violations in basketball including the double dribble (see page 13), traveling, and standing in the opponent's key for more than three seconds.

A basketball player's clothing is simple—a comfortable, loose-fitting vest and shorts and thick, cotton socks. Basketball boots offer lots of support and protection for the player's foot, especially around the ankle. Make sure your basketball footwear fits well and that the laces are tied securely with no trailing or flapping laces that could trip you.

These players perform a muscle stretch under the supervision of their coach. Basketball puts great strain on your body and its muscles, which is why warming up and stretching under the guidance of a coach is crucial to help prevent injuries.

A full-sized basketball has a circumference of 29 1/2–30 3/4 inches (75–78 centimeters) and weighs up to 1 1/2 pounds (650 grams).

The basketball hoop measures 17 3/4 inches (45 centimeters) in diameter and is suspended at a height of 10 feet (3.05 meters) from the floor. It is fitted to a large backboard, which allows players to bounce shots into the basket.

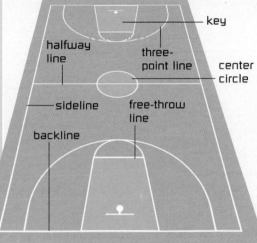

halfway line

key

three-point line

center circle

sideline

free-throw line

backline

The court

The markings on basketball courts may vary, but all courts have a center circle, a halfway line, and boundary markings (the sidelines and the backline at each end of the court). There is also a marked-out area in front of each basket, called the key.

This player is out of play because his left foot is over one of the sidelines. The other team will get the ball and restart the game with a throw from the sideline.

Topping up fluids during exercise, training, and while playing a game is essential if a player is to perform at his or her best. You should keep a water bottle by the side of the court or in your sports bag.

A player passes to his teammate from behind the backline to get the game going. A backline throw is used in two situations. The first is when the ball has touched or crossed the backline and is touched last by the attacking team. The second is when the attacking team has scored a basket.

STANCE AND PIVOTING

Receiving the ball calls for total concentration to watch the ball right into your hands. Once you have received the ball, you have plenty of options, especially if you get into the triple threat stance.

THE TRIPLE THREAT STANCE

The triple threat stance is so called because you can easily choose to make a pass, to dribble, or to shoot when you are in this position. Apart from giving you plenty of options, it can be difficult for a defender who does not know which of these threats to guard against.

PIVOTING

Frequently, you will receive the ball while you are on the move. There are two ways in which you can come to a stop. A stride stop (a "one-two" stop) is when one foot touches the floor before the other foot, and the first foot down is the pivot foot. A jump stop is when both feet land on the floor at the same time, and you can then choose your pivot foot. The pivot foot stays in the same place on the court, and you use the other foot to take steps around this pivot. Pivoting allows you to turn in both directions. It is an important skill because it can help you create space to pass or shoot.

The stance

This player is ready to receive the ball. His arms are out and his fingers slightly spread. He watches the ball carefully. As the ball arrives, he moves into the triple threat stance with his weight on the balls of his feet, his knees bent, and his head up.

Pivoting

1 The attacking player with the ball is closely marked. His pivot foot (his left) is planted.

2 He takes steps with his right foot to turn around, keeping balanced all the time.

3 He turns at the waist and brings the ball up to throw a chest pass to a teammate, who is free to receive the ball.

FAKES

Fakes are where you pretend to do one thing, but actually do something else. For example, you may fake a pass to your left, but quickly pivot and throw to your right. For a fake to work, the fake action has to be convincing to trick the defender. Then the actual move you want to make has to be completed rapidly before the opponent has recovered.

Fake-and-go

This attacker (left) looks as if he is going to shoot at the basket. The defender is convinced and gets his arms high in an attempt to block the shot. At the last moment, the attacker whips the ball down into his chest, turns, and performs a chest pass to his left.

1 This attacker performs a fake-and-go move. He starts by looking as if he is going to send a bounce pass to a teammate to his right.

2 The defender shifts his bodyweight and leans to that side to try to cover the pass, but the attacker quickly retracts the ball and brings it to his left side.

3 With the defender trying to recover his position, the attacker drives forward and toward the basket.

This attacker (right) fakes a pass and then goes for a shot. He leans outward and really looks as if he is about to throw a chest pass. The defender moves to cover the pass and lunges with his arms out to the side. As he does so, the attacker whips the ball back in and above his head to fire off a quick shot before the defender can recover.

9

PASSING

Passing is the quickest way to move the ball around the court. Passing can also be a low-risk way of getting the ball past defenders. Teams with excellent passers and good movement often create many chances to score baskets.

DID YOU KNOW?

John Stockton made more assists in the NBA than any other player before him or since—a massive 15,806 passes to players who went on to score.

PERFECT PASSING

There are many different types of pass. You need to make sure your receiver is expecting a pass and then send the ball to the ideal target position. If your receiver is moving, you will need to judge where he or she will be when the ball arrives.

You must also pass the ball with the right amount of force. A weak pass risks being intercepted, but overpowering a short pass can see the ball fly off the court or force your receiver into fumbling and dropping the ball. Playing a range of different passing drills can help sharpen your passing.

Here, you can see how the passer spreads his hands around the ball.

Chest pass

1 The chest pass is the most simple and common pass. This attacker has moved from the triple threat stance and brought the ball into the center of his chest.

2 The player's elbows are out wide and bent. As the player steps forward, the elbows snap straight and the ball is pushed out of the hands.

3 As the arms straighten, the attacker flicks his wrists to release the ball. The ball should fly straight to the receiver and not loop through the air.

Overhead pass

The overhead pass is useful as an immediate pass when you have caught the ball with your arms high up. The player first gets the ball directly above his head. His hands are around the sides and back of the ball, as with the chest pass. As he moves into the pass, he releases the ball with a snap of his wrists. His fingers first point forward and then down as he follows through.

JUDGMENT AND DISGUISE

Judging which pass to play at the right time is a great skill and only comes with lots of practice and match experience. One important factor is not to take too long with your pass so that the opposition can guess what is going to happen. This could allow an opponent to intercept your pass. The use of pivoting and faking to dribble, shoot, or pass in different directions are ways that can help to disguise your intended pass.

Simpler than the one-handed bounce pass, the two-handed bounce sees the passer aim for a point about two-thirds of the way to the receiver.

Bounce pass

1 The one-handed bounce pass with a stepover is a great way of passing the ball when marked closely. Here, the attacker starts to step with his nonpivot foot.

2 The passer turns his body as he completes his step so that most of his body is now between the defender and the ball. He has bent his legs to get lower and he is focused on the receiver.

3 The passer's hand begins to drive forward and down, aiming to bounce the ball at a point about two-thirds of the way toward the receiver.

4 The passer's arm straightens as the basketball is driven away. The defender has been cut out by the pass, which should rise to around hip level or slightly higher— a height that is easy for the receiver to gather.

DRIBBLING

Dribbling is simply moving around the court as you bounce the ball with one hand. Dribbling allows players to surge into different parts of the court and can end with a shot at the basket.

DRIBBLING BASICS

Good dribbling relies on smooth hand movements. You should build a good rhythm by pressing the ball down, not slapping it. Dribbling is a skill that definitely pays to practice in training and whenever you have a ball with you. As you improve your dribbling, you will be able to keep your head up so that you can see what is happening around you. You are allowed to swap hands in the middle of a dribble. However, you cannot catch the ball in both hands and then start dribbling again. This is called a "double dribble."

DID YOU KNOW?

The Argentinian men's team stunned many basketball fans at the 2004 Olympics by beating the U.S. team 89–81 during their semifinal. They then beat Italy in the final to win the gold medal.

The dribbler uses the top joints of the fingers and thumb, and not the palm of the hand to contact the ball.

Dribbling

1 The dribbler's body leans forward with knees bent and head up. He flexes his wrist and pushes the ball down and slightly in front of him.

2 As the ball leaves, his hand follows through in the direction of the ball's movement. The ball should bounce and rise to between knee and waist height.

3 The player collects the ball by letting his wrist rise with the ball's bounce to cushion the ball. The wrist then flexes again as he repeats the dribbling movement to send the ball down to the floor again.

DIFFERENT DRIBBLES

The basic dribble can be adjusted for different situations. A player can push the ball harder toward the floor and farther away from him when performing a power dribble. This is used when a player makes a fast break and there is a lot of court space free of opponents ahead of him. The reverse dribble uses a turn to change direction rapidly, and the crossover dribble can be used when a dribbler is on the move to unbalance a moving defender who is not too close.

This hand has twisted past 90 degrees to cradle the ball. This will result in a violation called a carry. Always keep your hand above the ball with your palm facing downward.

Crossover dribbling

The crossover dribble is a simple dribbling move where the ball is bounce passed between the two hands back and forth. The ball's path forms a "V" shape. Crossover dribbling can allow a moving dribbler the chance to drive to his or her left or right as a space opens up.

A crossover dribble

An official signals a double dribble violation. Possession of the ball will switch to the opposing team and the game will restart with a sideline throw.

Reverse dribbling

1 This attacker has been dribbling with his left hand but wants to change direction. He switches dribbling to his right hand.

2 He pivots around on his right foot, driving the ball with his right hand so that his body is protecting the ball.

3 The dribbler rolls around his opponent and may now choose to sprint away. Alternatively, he may now be able to see a teammate in a promising position.

Great passing and receiving skills need to be backed up by great movement around the court. Players both with and without the ball need to learn how to get free of opponents, get into space, and understand where promising positions are on the court.

DID YOU KNOW?

The NBA legend, Oscar Robertson, averaged over 30 points per game, every game for six seasons in a row.

Faking

1 The player in black is trying to get free of the defender, who is marking him closely. He fakes a move to his left.

2 The defender heads the same way, but the attacker makes a move to the right.

3 The attacker sprints forward as he makes eye contact with his teammate with the ball.

CHANGING PACE AND DIRECTION

You do not need to spend the whole game sprinting around at top speed to get free and into space. Changes of pace are often very effective. They tend to work best with a fake, where you pretend to head one way to unbalance a defender and then quickly head in a different direction. As you cut away, make sure you are looking up to see if you can receive a pass. Try and vary your directions and fakes during a game so that the defender is not sure what you will do next.

4 The attacker gets his arms up and out to receive a pass. He is now free of his marker and can look to pass, dribble, or shoot.

TARGET AREAS

A good place to be on court may seem to be anywhere that you are free of an opponent and in space, but this is not always the case. Being in space but in a position where your teammate with the ball cannot see you or cannot reach you is of little use. Taking a good position also applies to the player with the ball. For example, driving into a corner of the court may see you hemmed in by defenders and in a very difficult position to pass or shoot. Good basketball players try to get into a position where they have more than one option for their next move.

The attacker in black gets free by moving away from the player with the ball. He then sprints into space to receive a pass. This move is called a "V-cut."

Give-and-go

1 The give-and-go move is the equivalent of the one-two wall pass in soccer. The player with the ball spots his teammate moving to the side of a defender.

2 The player makes a quick pass to his teammate and as the ball leaves his hands, he sprints hard past his marker and into space to receive a return pass.

3 His teammate pivots and makes the pass to the other side of the defender, timing his release of the ball to allow for the first attacker's running speed.

Creating space

1 Sometimes, space can be created not for yourself but for a teammate. Here, an attacker cuts sharply to the side as if he is about to receive a pass.

2 The defender follows the attacker's move. The attacker has drawn the defender, creating a crucial space in the middle of the court.

3 The player on the ball reacts and drives into the gap left by the defender. He now has a clear run to the basket.

SCREENING

Creating space does not always involve one attacker cutting free of his marker. Players can work together to create space for each other using moves that legally block one or more defenders from heading where they want to. This is called screening.

DID YOU KNOW?

Manute Bol is the NBA's tallest-ever player. He played from 1985 to 1995 and was 7 1/2 feet (2.31 meters) tall.

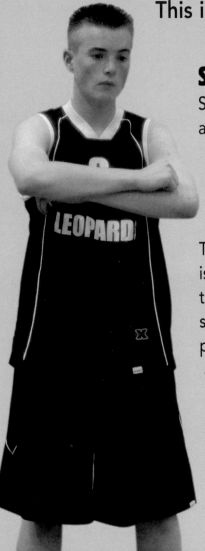

SETTING A SCREEN

Setting a screen relies on one attacker getting in a position and standing still before a defender can move into him or her. Many screens fail and end up with the referee signaling a foul, because the attacker has been slow to set up the screen and is still moving as the defender bumps into them.

The key to screening is picking a good place to stand. There is no point in setting a screen in a place that does not block the most likely path a defender wants to take. A player setting a screen has to be able to read the game well. The player with the ball who will benefit from the screen must also use the screen well, and ideally, move closely past his screening teammate.

A good screening stance (left) is with your feet wide apart. This makes it harder for the defender to get around you. Your arms should be held into your body and you must not grab hold of the defender.

This player (right) is in an incorrect screening stance since his foot is up off the ground. The referee will signal a foul. If the player's arms were out impeding the defender from moving, that would also be a foul.

1 The attacker on the left is about to set a simple screen to help protect his teammate with the ball who is dribbling past.

2 The player setting the screen makes sure that both of his feet are on the ground and that he is stationary before the defender moves into him.

3 The dribbler moves close to the screen his teammate has set. The defender's quickest path to challenge the dribbler is now blocked by the screener. The screening player has to stay still throughout the move until his teammate has dribbled past.

4 Here, the defender has given up his chase of the dribbler. Although some contact is allowed, the defender is not allowed to push the player setting the screen.

5 The screening player turns and follows the dribbler quickly toward the basket.

OFF-BALL SCREENING

There are lots of different screening moves, and the more experienced a player you become, the more screens you will be taught by your coach. One classic screen is to free a teammate without the ball to get into space to receive the ball. This screen move may be rehearsed in practice with the player aiming to get free by making a "V-cut" (see page 15).

This referee is signaling an illegal blocking action.

DEFENDING

Defending is about trying to regain possession of the ball as soon as possible and stopping the opposition from scoring. Defenders need individual skills, but they must work together as a team to put as much pressure on the opposition as possible.

MARKING OPPONENTS

Marking is guarding an opponent or an area of the court. In man-to-man marking, each player keeps close to and guards a single opponent. The defenders try to keep between their opponents and the basket at all times.

If defenders are guarding opponents with the ball, they look to harass and block passes or shots. Defenders have to be aware of opponents turning to drive past them or tricking them with a fake move. If they are guarding players without the ball, they have to be aware of where the ball is and be ready to cover any moves their opponents make.

Shot blocking
Most blocked shots require the defender to time his jump. This defender in white is preventing a scoring shot. He has shown excellent skill and timing to jump and block the ball without touching the attacker.

1 This defender in white is marking a player who has been dribbling but has stopped. The defender now knows that the attacker has only two options—shoot or pass.

Close marking

2 The defender gets close to his opponent with his knees bent and his arms up and out, ready for a block. As the attacker moves the ball from side to side, the defender should follow with his arms.

DEFENDING AWARENESS

During marking, defenders need to be aware of the game around them. A teammate may lose an opponent, who then sprints close to the basket. In this situation, you may decide to call a "switch," where you move to mark the free opposition player while your teammate takes your original opponent.

Staying aware has other benefits since you may spot a weak or poorly aimed pass that you can reach and intercept.

Jockeying

1 This defender in white is marking his opponent, who is dribbling the ball. The defender's arms are out wide.

2 He moves to cover the attack but does not cross his feet. Instead, he takes sliding or shuffling steps across the court.

3 The defender keeps between his opponent and the basket, forcing him to move toward the left-hand sideline.

4 The defender continues to move, always alert in case the attacker tries to drive past him down the sideline.

Stealing a pass

1 This defender in white has spotted a poor pass early and has decided to try and intercept the ball before it reaches the attacker.

2 He drives forward rapidly with his arms out to collect the ball before his opponent.

3 The player immediately begins a fast break toward the opposition basket. Interceptions are often great opportunities to turn defense into attack.

19

FOULS AND FREE THROWS

When fouls occur in basketball, they are signaled by the referee, counted against a player and can sometimes result in free throws being awarded to the fouled player's team. A free throw is an uncontested throw taken from in front of the basket. If it is successful, each free throw is worth one point.

DID YOU KNOW?

Reggie Miller holds the record for the most three-point baskets scored in NBA history. Throughout his career, he managed to score a total of 2,560.

Charge foul: The attacker in black with the ball has deliberately made a heavy contact with the body of a stationary defender. The referee will award a "charging foul" against him.

Slapping arms foul: The defender in white tries to get to the ball but is guilty of hitting the arms of his opponent. The referee will signal an "illegal use of hands foul" against the defender.

Shooting foul: This attacker in black is fouled as he shoots. If his shot is successful, he will get the two points and receive one free throw. If it was not, he will be awarded two free throws. If he was attempting a three-point shot, he would receive three free throws.

In FIBA rules, in addition to the free throw shooter, two additional attackers and three defenders are allowed to line up around the key.

PERSONAL AND TECHNICAL FOULS

There are two main types of foul—personal and technical. A personal foul involves some form of illegal contact made on an opponent. Examples include tripping or pushing opponents, or pulling their shirts. A technical foul occurs when a player or the team's coach is guilty of offenses that include interfering with a sideline throw or using offensive language or threats. A technical foul results automatically in two free throws to the opposition and possession of the ball from the halfway line.

FOUL PROCEDURE

When a referee signals a foul, he or she will also indicate which player the foul is against. That player should hold a hand up to aid the scorer. A player who reaches the foul limit during a game (six in the NBA, five in FIBA competitions) can no longer play in that game. Unlike many team sports, this does not mean that his side continues with one player less. Instead, a substitute can come onto the court to make up the numbers.

FREE THROWS

A free throw sees the player stand behind the free-throw line right in front of the basket and take a free shot. When a personal foul has occurred, the player fouled has to take the free throw. If a technical foul is signaled, any player can take the shots. Defenders and attackers stand around the edge of the key in set places. As the last free throw goes up, these players can move in to collect the ball if the shot is not successful.

Rebounding

As the thrower releases the ball on his last free throw, the players around the key can step into the key to try to secure a rebound. Here, the ball rebounds to the left with the attackers in black and defenders in white competing for the ball.

1 This player is using the "set shot" to take a free throw. His feet are shoulder-width apart with his toes and body pointing toward the basket. The player grips the ball with his shooting hand spread around the back of the ball and his elbow directly underneath the ball.

Free throw

2 The player bends at the knees and then extends his shooting arm as he rises. He pushes the ball away with his shooting arm, wrist, and fingers.

3 His wrist snaps forward as the ball flies away off the middle three fingers. The ball should rise nice and high above the basket, before dropping through the hoop.

JUMP AND HOOK SHOTS

The jump shot is a vital part of any player's game. Based on the set shot, it can allow you to shoot over a defender and reduce the risk of a block or interception. The jump shot can also be used for long-range, three-point attempts, and the hook shot is a more extravagant but useful shot technique.

SHOT CHOICE

The situation you face as you plan to shoot will determine what shot to use. If you are around the edge of the key and unmarked, a set shot may be the best option. If a defender stands in your way, a jump shot may be a better choice. A hook shot should be only when you are far from the basket. But if you are in the key and find your shooting arm farthest away from the basket, the hook shot can be effective.

The jump shot

1 This player is about to make a jump shot. His knees are bent and his back is straight. He has raised the ball just above his head, with his shooting hand spread around the bottom of the ball and his other hand on the top and side of the ball.

2 He springs up off both feet, driving straight upward using his legs. The elbow of his shooting hand stays directly underneath the ball as the arm straightens.

3 The arms straighten, and as they do, the supporting hand is removed from the ball. The ball is released at the top of the player's jump. The hands follow through with a flick of the wrists.

4 The ball should travel more upward than outward on its path toward the basket. The player looks to land on both feet, ready to react in case of a rebound.

SHOOTING DRILLS

Practice the various shooting techniques as often as possible. Repeat a series of shots from one point around the key, and make sure you hit the target a number of times before moving to another part of the key. Get your coach to work with you to improve your shooting.

THREE POINTS

The three-point line is an arc that is 21 feet (6.25 meters) away from the basket. The same technique used for the set shot or jump shot can be applied to three-point shooting. You should drive up strongly with your legs, and your body, hand, arm, and elbow must all stay aligned for the shot to be accurate.

Step back, jump shot

To create extra space to get a shot away over a marker, this attacker in black begins to step back. His pivot foot is his right, so he starts to step back with his left. As he does so, he leans back and brings the ball up into the shooting position, lining up his shot. The attacker moves into the jump shot, bending his knees to spring up. The defender lunges forward but the shooter's jump and his outstretched arms take the ball out of the defender's reach. The shooter releases the ball at the top of his jump.

From the front, you can see how this player (left) is focusing on the basket with his elbow bent and directly under the ball. The ball is being supported by the nonshooting hand.

The hook shot

1 A hook shot is a useful short-range shot made with the arm farthest away from the basket. The ball lies on the player's shooting hand.

2 The player starts to bring the ball up, releasing his supporting hand. His eyes look over his left shoulder, which is pointing at the basket.

3 He brings the ball up and over his head and releases it with a flick of his wrist. His shooting arm continues to follow through.

LAYUPS

Layups are driving plays toward the basket that end with a scoring chance from very short range. Because of the short distance from your shooting hand to the basket, layups often offer the easiest way of scoring.

LAYUP ACTION

A layup sees a player take one large stride into the key, and then leap up toward the basket to get as close as possible before trying to score. The player could have been dribbling beforehand or collected the ball from a pass. The attacker will try to time his or her movements to collect the ball in midair, take a stride, and then explode upward.

SHOT VARIATIONS

The most common layup shot method is overhand, where the ball is pushed upward by the hand, either to bounce off the backboard or to loop upward and straight into the hoop. The reverse layup (see below) makes use of the underhand method, where the ball sits on the hand and is lifted up into the basket. Top players also make use of the spectacular "slam dunk," where their hand is above the hoop and the ball is slammed down into the basket with force.

DID YOU KNOW?

In June 2006, the type of ball used in the NBA was changed for the first time in 35 years. The players complained bitterly about the new covering on the ball and within six months, the old type of leather ball was back in use.

Reverse layup

The reverse layup sees this player take his final stride underneath the basket. Springing up off his left foot, the player brings the ball up with both hands on the ball, then releases his nonshooting hand (his left) and hooks his right arm up and over his head. At the very top of his jump, his arm is fully extended upward with the ball sitting on his right hand. He judges the right amount of force to release the ball to bounce off the backboard and through the hoop.

1 The player completes a long stride into the key. The shot will be made with the arm nearest to the basket (his right).

2 The player powers off his left foot and springs up. He begins raising the ball, which is held in both hands.

3 The player stretches up and brings his arms fully above and slightly in front of his head.

The inner rectangle marked on the backboard can act as a useful target for a player making a layup. Players should aim for one of the top corners of this box to direct the ball into the hoop.

4 Watching the basket, the player releases the ball off his fingertips at the very top of his jump. He pushes the ball gently to bounce off the backboard and through the hoop. His wrist follows through after the shot.

5 The player lands on the balls of his feet. He continues to watch the ball in case it misses its target and bounces back.

LAYUP DRILLS

Layups require good rhythm and agility. They are often used as a warm-up drill before a game, and beginners should practice layups as often as possible from both sides of the basket. Beginners sometimes find it handy to split the move into two parts—the stride and jump up toward the backboard, and the jump up and shot from a still position. In time, you will get used to the angles you can bounce the ball off the backboard and how much force is required to send the ball into the basket.

JUMPING AND REBOUNDING

A basketball player often has to jump in a game, whether it is to contest the ball at a jump ball or to block a shot. Jumping is also an important part of the vital skill of rebounding—when players try to secure the ball after a shot has failed.

JUMP BALL

A jump ball is used to start a game of basketball. It involves the referee throwing the ball into the air and one player from each side leaping to make contact with the ball, in order to pat it down to a teammate nearby.

DID YOU KNOW?

At the 2000 Olympics, the U.S. women's player, Yolanda Griffith, managed a record 70 rebounds.

1 These two players contest a jump ball at the start of the game. They stand inside the center circle and the referee throws the ball straight up in the air.

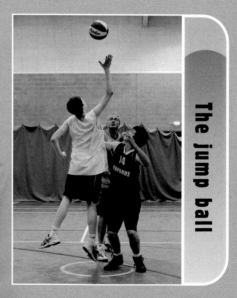

The jump ball

2 The two players jump to try to tap the ball down and toward one of their teammates standing outside of the center circle. Neither player can catch the ball or tap it more than twice, until it has been touched by a player outside of the center circle.

REBOUNDING

Rebounding is one of the few skills used by both defenders and attackers. Rebounding involves a jump to try to gather the ball that has deflected or cannoned off the backboard or hoop. Before the jump, however, players must use experience and judgement to anticipate a rebound occurring and where the ball is likely to head. They must then get into a strong position early, ahead of any opponents. As a rebound is secured, the rebounder has to decide on his or her next move. A defender may look to get the ball out of the key with a safe pass to the side. This is known as an outlet pass. An attacker may be able to fake and put up another shot or pass quickly to a teammate in a good position to shoot themselves.

Two players wrestle for control of the ball. As long as neither of them fouls the other, the referee is likely to signal a held ball and one team will be awarded possession with a sideline throw. This possession is determined on an alternating basis.

Rebounds

1 As an attacker has tried a shot on goal, the defender in white pivots around to face the basket without fouling his opponent.

2 The defender uses a wide stance to make it harder for the attacker to get around him. This is known as blocking or boxing out.

3 The players watch the ball as it rebounds off the hoop and backboard. The defender predicts where the ball will travel next and moves in closer to the basket.

4 The defender springs up and stretches his arms to take the ball as high as possible. As soon as he has caught the ball, he will gather it into his chest safely.

5 The defender lands, pivots quickly, and sends an outlet pass to a teammate in space near the sideline.

6 With his pass safely on its way, the defender should now move quickly to get free of his opponent since his side now starts to build an attack.

TEAM PLAYS

Many of the techniques so far have been either individual skills or moves performed by two or three teammates working together. There are also a number of tactics involving all or almost all of the whole team on court, both in attack and defense.

COMMUNICATION

For team plays to work, all players in a side should practice the moves so that they know what their precise roles are. Communication with teammates is vital in many basketball skills, but especially in team plays. Keep your head up and your ears open. A sudden instruction given as a call or hand signal by a teammate could be the difference between the team play working or not.

The players in black are trying to make a fast break from under their own basket and catch the other team out of position. One of the team sprints out wide along a sideline and will turn his head shortly to see if a long pass could reach him.

Calling for a pass

This player is in space and signaling for a pass to come to him. Do not get frustrated if sometimes your teammates do not react quickly enough or choose not to pass to you. Instead, you should continue to work hard to get into good positions to receive the ball.

PRESSURE DEFENSE

Defending can be about forcing a team into making a poor pass, a fumble, or a hurried shot. It can also be about making the attacking team run out of time, either when they are trying to get the ball out of their back court or make a shot before the shot clock runs out. A full court press is an aggressive team play where defenders mark attackers one-on-one in the opponent's back court. The aim is to stop opponents from getting the ball out of their back court within the eight-second time limit. It is also sometimes used when the defending team are a couple of points behind and game time is running out.

The team in white are performing an aggressive full court press on the opposition. By marking really tightly, they are denying opportunities for passing and are trapping the player with the ball on his backline. If they can keep the other side in their backcourt for eight seconds, the ball will be awarded to them.

Fake shot and pass

1 These two attackers have made a fast break and are in a two-versus-one situation close to the basket. This is a superb opportunity to score. The player with the ball plants his feet and moves into the triple threat stance.

2 The one defender moves to mark the player with the ball as he appears to be about to take a shot at the basket. The other attacker, though, is in a good position to receive a pass.

3 The player has faked a shot but instead passes quickly to his teammate. The defender has been cut out by the pass, leaving the second attacker free.

4 The second player chooses to shoot straight for the basket. He also has the option of driving toward the basket to perform a layup.

Glossary

assist A pass leading directly to a scoring shot.

backboard The large board that is fixed behind and above the basket. Players can bounce shots off the backboard to score.

back court The half of the court that a team is defending.

blocking The illegal obstruction of a player.

cut A fast movement made by an attacker without the ball to find space.

double dribble A violation that occurs when a player dribbles the ball, catches it, and then dribbles again.

drive A fast, aggressive dribble toward the basket.

fast break Quick movement by a team with the ball down the court in order to get behind the defense and score a basket.

front court The half of the court that the team with the ball is attacking.

full court press A type of close defense applied over the whole basketball court by one team.

hoop Another term for the basket.

jump ball A move that starts every game and occurs when a referee tosses the ball into the air between one player from each side.

key The area around a basket in which attacking players are only allowed to stand for three seconds at a time. It is also known as the three-second area.

layup A short-range scoring move where a player steps in toward the basket, jumps and either aims the ball straight into the basket or bounces it off the backboard first.

man-to-man defense A way of defending where each defender marks an individual opponent.

offense Another term for attacking with the ball.

overtime An extra period of playing time added at the end of normal time if the scores are level.

rebounding Jumping and collecting the ball after it has bounced off the backboard or hoop.

screen An attacking play where an attacker uses their body to legally delay an opponent from reaching where he or she wants to head on the court.

shot clock A clock that shows the time a team with the ball has left to shoot at the basket.

slam dunk A spectacular scoring move where a player leaps high and drives the ball into the basket with force.

steal Winning the ball from an opponent fairly.

traveling A violation when a player takes too many steps after catching the ball.

turnover Losing possession without having taken a shot.

V-cut A fake play where a player fakes to move in one direction but moves in the opposite direction in order to get free to receive a pass.

Diet and nutrition

Basketball is a high-energy sport that is best played by players who have prepared well. Part of this preparation is to have good fitness levels and to eat a healthy diet. Try to avoid fast foods with high levels of fat and sugar, and make sure you eat a meal at least a few hours before a match or practice, so that your body can start digesting it.

A good, balanced diet contains foods that are relatively low in sugars and fats but high in protein, carbohydrates, and contain healthy amounts of fiber, vitamins, and minerals, which enable your body to grow and function at its best. For long practices or a series of games in a row, pack a light snack, such as fruit, a granola bar, or a sandwich, and drink plenty of water to replace the fluids lost as you work hard.

Books

Basketball Skills and Drills, Jerry Krause
(Human Kinetics Publishers, 2007)

Youth Basketball Drills, Burrall Paye
(Human Kinetics Publishers, 2000)

Web Sites

Due to the changing nature of Internet links, PowerKids Press has developed an online list of Web Sites related to the subject of this book. This site is updated regularly. Please use this link to access this list:
www.powerkidslinks.com/best/basket

INDEX